CW01650298

Tony McIntosh is a West Norfolk resident. He has written a previous Anthology of verse entitled Assorted musings. He retired two years ago having previously worked in the civil service, NHS as a trained Psychiatric nurse and latterly as a home carer in social care. He enjoys being with family, including his grandchildren. His hobbies include walking, cooking, ornithology, choir singing and being a regular congregant at his local church. He also enjoys going to musical gigs with a preference for folk music. He also did voluntary work as a narrator for Talking newspapers.

In previous years, he funds raised for charities including the Anthony Nolan Trust, RNLI and the Samaritans for whom he was a volunteer in the 1970s.

Heartfelt thanks to my wife Christine and my family for supporting me to put pen to paper. This has spurred me on in my project!

Tony McIntosh

A Bardic Melange

Austin Macauley Publishers™
London • Cambridge • New York • Sharjah

A CIP catalogue record for this title is available from the British Library.

ISBN 9781035863891 (Paperback)
ISBN 9781035863907 (ePub e-book)

www.austinmacauley.com

First Published 2024
Austin Macauley Publishers Ltd®
1 Canada Square
Canary Wharf
London
E14 5AA

Sincere gratitude is owed to the publisher, Austin Macauley, for enabling this book to come to life. Their professionalism and dedication in their endeavours is second to none.

You Are the Glue

At the start of our adventure as we erred and strayed
Not one word of censure, nor disapproval by you was made
You waited and watched as we disappeared from view
But your invisible force returned us, lest we became frayed
You did it because you are the glue

As life progressed, and from our nests we wandered
Along many highways, we twisted and meandered
At all junctures you were aware, put simply, you knew
You mended our bodies and to our every whim you pandered
You reassembled us because you are the glue

At times our beliefs may have started to falter
"No problem" you assured us as you applied the halter
You gently guided us back 'ere our lives went askew
And brought us before the heavenly altar
You repaired our faith because you are the glue

We came back to the fold, tails between legs
Contrition expressed as in supplication we begged
We confessed to becoming embroiled in a stew
Then you offered us a drink from the heavenly keg
A calming, relaxing yet intoxicating brew

When you hung from that cross, not once were you blue
You said, "Forgive them Father for they know not what they do"
You implored us all not to be sad or to crack
For on the third day, you proclaimed, "I will be back"
"To redeem the world for, 'tis true, I am the glue"

Dedicated to Pearl, R.I.P, 18th May 2023

Pardon My Padron!

I've travelled far to this remote location
E'en though it's part of the same vast nation
The views are awesome, the setting serene
The air is invigoratingly clean

I could be anywhere in this world
With drama yet to unfurl
I calm my body as I take a breather
Allowing myself to float into the ether

I've come here to celebrate a milestone in my life
Away from the rat race and associated strife
God made this place, the true meaning of Mother Lode
A veritable El Dorado, removed from humanity's well-trodden road

I'm relaxed and chilled, I could stay here forever
The still, calm voice inside tells me, "Never say never"
But needs must, I don't intend to be rude
It's time for a repast, a cornucopia of food

The eaterie is welcoming, the staff well-trained
As each course of the taster menu is painstakingly explained
The fare looks invitingly pleasurable
The restaurant's acclaim is immeasurable

Thus, I settle down with my partner; so far so good!
The ambience is "cool" as I take a sip from my "Bud"
It's time to tuck into the garden plate
Little did I know, as I awaited my fate!

The greens are chargrilled and well-presented
The peppers are mild, so I readily consented
I sampled one but the heat was intense
It knocked my head back. This made no sense

I struggle for breath, my gullet afire
Tonight, I won't be singing in the choir!
I crave for fresh and plenty of water
I just want to feel like I oughtta!

I rise to the challenge and complete the courses
Those chefs sure produce some incredible sauces
I'm exhausted but no longer plagued by impending doom
As I hit the sack in my bothy room

Next day I still felt tender but calm
Let's face it, I've no long-lasting harm!
But, Pedro, pardon my Padron from Galicia, Spain
For I won't be devouring you again!

Granddaughter

I first saw you at 6 hours old
A tiny bundle almost too precious to hold
With your voluminous black hair sprouting up from your head
Stubbornly refusing to flatten, it was said

As the months went by you learned to walk
We wondered what you might say when you started to talk
Your Christening arrived in which you showed spirit most blithe
Who would you crawl to first? Me or my wife?

Crawl you did not. You took faltering paces
There was no hurry, you weren't at the races
You chose Grandad as you stretched out your arm
There was no way he'd let you fall into harm

At home, you cackled and laughed
You ran around at bath time. You weren't daft!
Your boundless energy knew no limits
Did you sleep at night? It took hours, not minutes!

Aged nearly 4 you moved with your mother
To a new home, sadly without a sister and brother
You settled down well and soon started school
You mixed with your peers as a general rule

Ever the extrovert, you danced on stage
Showing precocity, way ahead of your age
Gyrating away to Katrina and the Waves
You needed no props, neither sticks nor staves
Aged almost 6, you went on holiday with mum
"Down under", what an adventure. No need to feel glum
You stayed for a month in this far-off land
Meeting new folks with several trips planned

Back home you changed schools and had even more fun
You were good at sprinting as all the races you won
You made many friends and did well in class
However, Primary school education couldn't last

Time for "Big school", different topics to learn
Even though you still had energy to burn
You had to buckle down. You had no choice
There'd be plenty of time in future for boys!

You passed your exams and got accepted by the College
You stayed local. Why travel to Norwich?
You buckled down to your business studies
With a conscientious band of buddies

You passed your driving test and got your own "wheels"
Grandad's taxi service is defunct. You now know how he feels!
You have a boyfriend. You both have ambitions
Not too long now before you make important decisions

And so, this tale ends as you look to the future
But, for now, be grounded, not too attached to your computer
Enjoy yourself, carpe diem, seize the day
You wouldn't want it any other way!

Our Hero

Our hero was born in a small market town
Of that, we know for certain
His surroundings never got him down
As he regularly peered through the curtain

By far he was the youngest of four
The new kid on the block
His siblings would play with him on the floor
Until bedtime; always 8 o'clock

Sadly, his mother died, with our hero aged one
This could have left him rueful
His much older sister took the mantle of mum
Years later, with him, she'd be truthful

His childhood was sheltered but rarely glum
His family spoiled him madly
He referred to his sister, loyally, as mum
They all gelled ever so gladly

He tried hard at school and had a few mates
They got involved in some right proper capers!
Playing down by the railway gates
Luckily, they were never named in the papers

His dad worked hard to instil self-belief.
He taught our hero the meaning of manners
To avoid getting into scraps and mischief
His reward? A pocket full of tanners!

Our hero left school at 14, the norm for that time
He quickly settled down to employment
He enjoyed fags, beer, whisky and lime
Which all added to life's enjoyment

War soon broke out. Hitler's stance was evil
The recruitment sergeant came a' calling
Everyone thought that the Fuhrer was the devil
Our hero considered him appalling

Off then, with his regiment, to Normandy's shores
Did our hero have time to be scared?
He probably was, but he did it because
Regarding freedom and justice, he cared

The campaign was exhausting and tiring
He witnessed sights nobody should espy
However, this was no time for crying
Even though, to his regiment, he'd soon say goodbye

He was medically discharged on doctor's orders
Never to return to action
But to leave his comrades, returning to the UK borders
Left him with bitter/sweet satisfaction

In the early fifties, he met a sweet lady
Shy, diffident but pretty
Our hero's intentions were anything but shady
To lose her would be such a pity!

After a year of romance, they did marry
It was a time to commit forever
Our hero ensured he did not tarry
They were wed until the twelfth of never
The years flew by, three children were bred

Finances were tight, the belts were tightened
But, after all, never let it be said
They would never be frightened

Our hero had the ambition to become self-employed
He aspired to own a business by forty
The dream came true; he was overjoyed
They celebrated as his wife poured tea

It was a labour of love, things didn't come easy
Would he be able to make ends meet?
The very notion could have made him feel queasy
He soldiered on, eventually landing on his feet

The venture became a success, it's safe to say
Customers returned again and again
But after 28 years it was time to call it a day
Our hero needed to remain sane!

Retirement was rewarding with holidays galore
North, South, East and West
When asked, of all the places he'd seen
He stressed that Egypt was, by far, the best!

A myriad of hobbies in which to partake
Gardening, Scottish dancing and touring
Many a bottle of wine he'd make
Life, assuredly, was not boring!

After 66 years of married bliss
His dearly beloved departed this earth
He never thought it would come to this
He'd truly understood love's worth
Our hero was bereft, not wanting to be alone
He just needed to feel loved by his kin
By his sorrow, he was savagely thrown
Surely there'd be room at the Inn?

His family rallied to ensure his needs were met
They couldn't leave him in such a quandary
With failing sight and memory, how could he forget?
He needed meals and someone to do his laundry

His health worsened, to hospital he went
Something had to give
He struggled to articulate. We knew what he meant
He just wanted somewhere to live

Aged 96, our hero's batteries expired
Old Father Time had called his number
For several years he'd looked increasingly tired
And often asked when he'd be in final slumber

We miss you Dad, our hero
You were always there to land an ear
Over a beverage in Café Nero
For now, we'll settle for a heavenly beer!

Sailing Too Close to the Wind

You've far exceeded your 15 minutes of fame
It's been one long extravagant game
The vultures now circle, too many to count
The pressure verily begins to mount
As you find yourself playing the end game

They say there's no smoke without fire
As you tread the tightrope wire
The chickens are coming home to roost
As the hangman tightens his noose
But you protest that you are no liar

The media created quite an inventory
With reports that included lewd, alleged, stories
You'd better be quick
Before the mud, it doth stick
To reclaim your earlier glories

But, my friend, you'd best prepare your defence
As all becomes increasingly tense
You'll need good representation
To redeem your dwindling reputation
Through the eyes of the camera lens

Your comments and behaviour did frequently shock
Characterised by flamboyance, truly baroque
You see, your humour was outdated
With your wit, less serrated
The roosting birds have landed on the dock
You assumed that you were a gift from above
With personality and charm that the fair sex would love
You proclaimed that it was all a "lark"
Seems you often overstepped the mark
Yet still you utter "It wasn't me guv!"

You see, that's the problem with fame
You, by your power and lust, knew no shame
You enticed and enchanted
Taking those maidens for granted
Ultimately, with no one else to blame

Your employers didn't appear to flinch
As you took several yards, not just an inch
Savile should have proved the watershed
But you continued to take women to bed
Far removed from the Christmas Grinch!

Don't forget when girls say NO
That means red for stop, not green for go
Respect their wishes
Be more judicious
Instead of causing tears to flow

However, many dirty deeds were done
As you had many days "in the sun"
So, prepare your case well
As you await the final bell
Since the quest for justice has now begun!

Who Is This Guy?

He has such incredible strengths
To help you, he will go to extreme lengths
Nothing, to him, is too much trouble
If you are at the bar, he'll buy you a double!

But who is he, this mystery dude?
Why is he never in a mood?
Where was he raised, if only we knew?
How did he live? Give us a clue!

They say that he hailed from a Middle east land
His life was pre-destined with great things planned
His beginnings were humble, his parents not wealthy
Though they ensured that he remained healthy

It soon became apparent he was a man on a mission
In between, he'd take his acquaintances fishing!
These allies would become vital to his life's work
Much to be done, with him they'd not shirk

His Commander in chief gave him instruction
To save the earth from apocalypse and destruction
To spread peace and love wherever he'd go
By his teachings, the answers he'd show

This redoubtable man gathered his assistants
To spread the gospel with little resistance
They were taught the parables in a timely fashion
In which, this great man displayed an infinite passion

These Acolytes witnessed the healing of the lame and sick
What joy to see the leper jettison his stick
Such acts were the work of one so-kind
Restoring sight to those who were blind

This miracle worker went out to sea
To help procure fish from Galilee
His workers were stunned by this amazing act
It sealed any doubts. What they beheld was fact!

Everywhere he went, he drew a great horde
Of people curious to see this Lord
So eager were they, this man, to meet
That they threw themselves down, prostrate at his feet

The Gospel was spread. That's all that mattered
However, this man was not easily shattered
He continued his quest to disperse the good news
And succeeded in eliminating people's blues

The fly in the ointment was the dismissive Pilate
A sceptical, disdainful, man who would not keep quiet
He condemned our great man in a Kangaroo court
With no shred of evidence ever sought

Our hero was made to convey his cross
Up to that hill, as we feared a great loss
Oh ye, of little faith, did you think he was gone?
For, on the third day, the sun resplendently shone

Our saviour was back, his sacrifice made
Light restored from the previous shade
He said, "Did you think I would forsake you?"
"Now let's crack on, for there's work to do!"

The Arbiter in Black

Who'd be a ref, Jeff?
An important task, don't you think?
They blow their whistles with all their breath
Whilst the players "kick up a stink"

Look at the linesman, he's raising his flag
The striker is "one on one" with the keeper
He smashes the ball into the onion bag
Yet is it really the time to shout "Eureka?"

The ref holds his hand, cupped to his ear
V.A.R is holding its adjudication
"You see that linesman over there?"
"Let him advise, we're on our Play station!"

What does the ref do now? After all, he's in charge
Or so we're given to understand
The opposing boss shouts out "By and large,
I think you're taking payments underhand!"

The ref walks across to the disgruntled boss
A red card is immediately brandished
"You imply I'm a cheat, but I don't give a toss
To the dressing room, you are banished

The goal is disallowed. All hell breaks loose
Fights break out all over the field
From the terraces spurts forth a chorus of boos
Look out, ref. Keep your eyes peeled

"That's it" says the ref, "I'm abandoning the match
I've had enough of this nonsense for now
My report to the league I will promptly despatch
Of that, you have my vow"

So, who'd be a ref? That's the question to ponder
Do they do it from the goodness of their heart?
Let's face it, they must often wonder
Why this job, they ever did start

Nevertheless, refs are essential to overseeing games
Without them, anarchy might rule
There's no need to resort to calling them names
To do so just renders you a fool!

These guys are deserving of our respect
So, before you get out your claws
Learn the rules, 'cos it's the least we'd expect
In the interpretation of the game's laws

"So, who'd be a ref Jeff", I hear you implore
It takes guts, fitness and endeavour
If you think you're ready to come to the fore
You've got to be canny, impartial but clever!

White, Black or Gray?

She had two men to choose from, lucky Miss White
She had much to ponder. Would she pick right?
She had to select from Messrs Gray or Black
To whom would she deliver the sack?

Black was named Jack, Gray known as Ray
But would Miss White decide today?
She had much to cogitate overnight
She must not allow herself to feel contrite

As she hunkered down for the night
Her future seemed overwhelmingly bright
She poured herself a stiff Armagnac
As ever, partial to a good Cognac

She mused that her future would be good craic
Good job they didn't live in Iraq!
She lay down and perused her almanack
On the morrow, she'd go for a hack

Her fondness for horses would help keep her sane
Come sunshine, wind or refreshing rain
She oft gave the impression of being quite fey
Verily, this would not be the case today

She wrestled her conscience with all her might
Gradually she determined her plight
Her steed emitted an ear-splitting neigh
As, at that juncture, she did earnestly pray

As she cantered along that track
She resolved there'd be no turning back
Her horse then slowed, as if wading through clay
As the mount returned to the highway

She started to sing the ballad, “Yesterday”
Wondering which beau would bring her “Milk Tray”
She made her decision before her nag took flight
For now, Miss White was feeling “high as a kite!

She’d decided, though the decision was tight
Finally, she had seen the light
Young Ray had been in many a melee
He was the first to step into any affray

Master Black worked climbing many a chimney stack
Miss White thought courage Jack did not lack
For her Jack was ahead of the pack
He would certainly cover her back

Forsooth, she must approach Ray Gray
There’d be no time like today
She hoped her explanation would not appear trite
Or that Ray would Jack not smite

Ray took the news well. He was quite polite
He did not want to become embroiled in a fight
The best man had won. There’d be no flak
As Ray heartily congratulated Jack!

No longer was Miss White on the shelf or rack
The rest of her days she would spend with Jack
Ray would resume his employ on a brewery dray
For Miss White, she had the final say. Yay!

Premier Bosses

The Anfield boss, Herr Klopp
Was famed for getting in a strop
He'd shout at the officials
For blowing their whistles
'Cos he wanted his team at the top

The Gunners have Mikel Arteta
He has made the Arsenal play better
He really does care
That his team shows flair
And to be the league's pace-setters

At first Geordie gaffer, Eddie Howe
Looked worried with a furrowed brow
But you should see him today
With his team's stylish play
He's not so fretful now!

Hammers' head honcho David Moyes
Is proud of his claret and blue boys
They play with panache
As the fans enjoy a bash
Such is the cacophony of noise

The Brighton head coach de Zerbi
Is very chipper and chirpy
The games he loves the most
Are played on the south coast
Especially a local derby
Brentford guv'nor, Thomas Frank
Likes to have points in the bank
The guy is no fool
In interviews, he's "cool"
He doesn't want his team walking the plank

Notts Forest head man Steve Cooper
Doesn't want his side to play a blooper
He demands plenty of finesse
As his team tried their best
And for the fans to shout out "super"

Wolves manager Gary O'Neill
Arranges his team's pre-match meal
Plenty of carbs such as pasta
To make his players run faster
As they put their shoulders to the wheel

The name Ange Postecoglou
To pronounce will surely bamboozle you
Spurs are on the way up
Sure to win the cup
Such is the magic of this guru

That wily Spaniard, Marco Silva
Runs Fulham, down by the Thames river
They play with aplomb
Like last night of the proms
With football to make your spine shiver!

The Downs

Let me introduce to you some rustic folk
A family almost financially broke
They go by the unfortunate surname Down
Between them, they can barely summon half a crown

There is old man, Sid, wife Ida and sons Ben and Bob
The boys struggled to find a meaningful job
No wonder that Sid always sported a frown
With old Ma Ida heading for a nervous breakdown

Sid drove a tractor and ploughed the earth, brown
Backwards and forwards across uneven ground
He loved his job as down the lanes he wound
Singing along to the tune "Homeward Bound"

Sid planned to meet the boys after work
Before daylight descended into murk
Ben and Bob met him in the "Rose & Crown"
Sid's frown lifted as he yelled "I've discovered a pound!"

Back home, Ida was sat in her tatty old gown
Listening to Diana Ross. She loved Motown!
Before that, she struggled to find a noun
You see, she loved watching the programme "Countdown"

Ida wished she could afford to go to town
But sadly, the place was so rundown
She looked down to Rufus, the mangy old hound
He just lay asleep, barely making a sound
Ida grew restless. Where would her men be found?
By her menfolk, she increasingly felt let down
She vowed there'd be one hell of a crackdown
She donned her shoes and walked round and round

She went up and over the nearby mound
Until those wretched males she found
She determined that there'd be a showdown
As she caught them supping in the "Rose & Crown"

She cried "Look at you, Sid. You resemble a clown
With your reddened nose, as your sorrows you drown
As for you layabouts Bob and Ben
I've told you buggers again and again"

"You are adults now, both fully grown
By this stage, our nest you should have flown
It's no good grumbling and emitting a groan
Get back home; cut the grass. Long time since it was mown"

Before further words old Ida could speak
The boys resolved for employment to seek
Before too long as time had flown
They both procured jobs, so Ida would not moan!

Eventually, family fortunes began to turn round
No more would their name be one of renown
Bob chopped down trees. To sea Ben did sail
Which brings us to the end of this abject tale!

Thanks Elton!

Oh Elton, Elton, the music was belting
The sun had set but you had our hearts melting
Your back catalogue was performed with panache
Smoothly delivered like chocolate ganache

You tinkled the ivories cleanly and true
No mistaking it was you
Aided and abetted by Bernie's lyrics
A night for the purists and musical critics

Your timing was perfect, singing a joy
Not bad for a Pinner, Northwest London boy!
How you remembered the words is astounding
As, simultaneously, your piano took a pounding!

The verses resonated and sounded just right
In "Someone saved my life tonight"
The words struck a chord in this emotional song
Misty eyed we all sang along

"Candle in the wind," always a favourite
You could tell that the audience craved it
"Philadelphia Freedom," such a stirring tune
Left fans feeling over the moon

You upped the tempo with "Crocodile rock"
A classic from your seventies stock
Then came "Saturday night's alright for fighting"
Provocative, as expected, but ever-exciting
The music score to "I'm still standing"
Had us air guitarists joining in the jamming
Not wanting your band to slack
With gusto erupted, "The bitch is back"

The faster beat of “Pinball wizard”
Proved that you were no lounge room lizard
The effort in your voice really showed
When you played “Goodbye yellow brick road”

It was one of the safer bets
That you would play “Bennie and the jets”
Back in 1976 when you headed the chart
With the timeless “Don’t go breaking my heart”

And as for the number I’d readily choose
“I guess that’s why they call it the blues”
The meaning and poignancy and so, so strong
No less the classic, immortal, “Your song!”

The ballads “Tiny dancer” and “Daniel”
Were just as sweet as a puppy Spaniel.
Equally sounding as pleasant and nice
Were the moving “Nikita” and “Sacrifice”

Drawing to a close, sung in perfect key
“Don’t let the sun go down on me”
To conclude and played with consummate elan
What else, but the epic “Rocket man”

Medical Woes

I devour pills for my ills
I take potions to aid my motions
My body aches, my bones do creak
It's been the same for many a week

Phoning the surgery is quite an ordeal
Just to explain how I physically feel
Eventually, a voice breaks through on the line
"Sorry. Appointments all gone. Ring another time!"

So, I give up and make do with the pain
With arthritis exacerbated by cold and rain
My health dictates that I no longer drive
The pain returns, cutting through like a knife

The Emergency Department is always busy
Just sitting there makes me feel dizzy
So much activity. What's it all for?
Hey look, someone else has checked in at the door

Receptionists, Nurses, and Doctors all look stressed
As they wearily explain they are all hard-pressed
But no! Another emergency takes precedence
At this rate, I'll soon be taking up residence!

So, forgive me I consider that by and large
I'm going to take my self-discharge
A taxi is called. I'm off home to my bed
To "God's waiting room", 'cos I'll soon be dead!

The Cooks' Tale

There lived a family down by the brook
Wally, Molly, Dolly, Holly and Ollie Cook
Old man, Wally, worked driving a truck
He didn't half curse when his sat-nav got stuck!

Dolly, one morning, with rage she shook
As Holly, her sister, the hair dryer she took
Young Ollie, he sniggered, laughing in the nook
For he aspired in future to pilot a Chinook

The poor old chickens in the coop did cluck
As old Ma Molly, their feathers did pluck
She liked to do everything by the book
As the startled poultry scratched around in the muck

On his way home many vehicles Wally overtook
Driving so erratically that the lorry it shook
The "Old Bill" stopped him. He'd run out of luck
They didn't let him off the hook

Back home, Wally told Molly "I'm no crook"
E'en though road legislation I mistook
Does that mean we can't now go to Kirkuk?
Or Morocco to visit markets or a Souk?

Molly exhorted "With you doth stop the buck"
Wally contemplated this as he tucked into not chicken but duck
A meal of which he wished he hadn't partook
He cried "I think I'm going to puke. Yuk"

He ran outside and exclaimed "Gadzooks"
"I'll have to give my dinner to the circling rooks"
Although this repast he had now forsook
He cared not how silly he might now look. Life sucks!

Childhood Holiday Memories

The aroma of fry-ups, especially bacon
Guaranteed to stop the belly from achin'
Cooked atop a rudimentary hob
We used to say, "Just the job!"

The caravan was supposed to be four berth
Who cared? Squeezing in five caused great mirth
No portable television in those halcyon days
Just sounds and music as the transistor radio played

Radio 2 was the grown-up's first choice
Us youngsters preferred Johnnie Walker's voice
The latter spun records on "Caroline"
Crackling sounds down the air wave's line

Walks with our dads were always a blast
A couple of miles, no need to go fast
Up the fern-bedecked hill, then back down below
Waiting at a bridge. Would the steam train show?

On through the woods, to the campsite ahead
Laughing and joking, we could've raised the dead!
Destination café for sweets and a bottle of pop
We didn't want the enjoyment to stop

Times at the amusement arcade spending those coppers
We won sixpence, now nothing could stop us!
Buying Marvel comics at the caravan park store
I could be Superman, but I can't get off the floor!
Power balls that bounced high into the sky
Balsa wood aeroplanes, how on earth did they fly?
"Dinky" cars, Matchbox toys that cost two and six
Whiled away time, if we got in a fix

Chips on the promenade straight from the bag
With dad in the background smoking a fag!
Down to the boating lake with our model yachts
Always one of our favourite spots

Outings to Great Yarmouth, ever a joy
So much to take in for a girl or a boy
The fairground was enormous for a day tripper
"Can I go again on the Big Dipper?"

A trip to a show amongst the bright lights
Mike Yarwood was amusing and the hilarious Barron Knights
The Pavilion theatre overlooking the sea
Provided hours of unrestrained family glee

Afternoons on the beach with the sun always shining
Dad's bringing the ice creams. Immaculate timing!
The holiday would soon come to an end
"Oh gosh!" A postcard to Nan I didn't send!
Never mind, I bought her an ornament gift
Hopefully, this will give her a "lift"

Back home again, when's the next vacation?
I guess we'll just have to be patient
No matter, those memories are all "in the bank"
Enabled by our parents. It's them we should thank!

World Cup 1966

Alf Ramsey had long since predicted an England victory
It would be years until his speech, valedictory
He'd fine-tuned the players to peak condition
There would be no words of contrition

Approaching the tournament, we were so excited
But for us fans would it be a case of love unrequited?
Such fears would soon prove unfounded
Ramsey's tactics would not leave us confounded

Schools taught us about each competing nation
The geography, flags and cultures of each location
The curriculum seemed adapted for the World Cup
We kids were enthralled like an ecstatic pup

And, so, the tournament eventually commenced
All would soon make eminent sense
Although it featured just 32 games
In no time we would recognise famous names

England started off with a draw
With a display that wouldn't drop one's jaw
The next two games would seal the deal
As our boys saw off Mexico and France for real!

So, to the last eight against Argentina at Wembley
This very notion could make your knees go trembly
Our opponents tried to kick us off the field
The ref sent off Rattin and the South Americans did yield
Hurst scored the goal to win the match
Who'd be next for England to despatch?
Portugal, with Eusebio, would be the next meeting
This slick side would not want to be beaten

England prevailed; their wish was met
Bobby Charlton firing two goals into the net
Eusebio replied once, but all in vain
In a World Cup, we would never see him again

Thus, to the final, where West Germany lay in wait
Ramsey's prediction; the result of fate
A hundred thousand fans packed into the ground
Dear Wembley had never heard such a sound!

Rattles rattling, flags waving
Expecting success that the country was craving
The Germans, though, would be no pushover
They yearned to be the ones rolling in clover

Onto the game, an intriguing tussle
What would decide it, brain, brawn or muscle?
Those dastardly Germans broke through first
Not expecting the equaliser from Hurst

Peters later put England into the lead
Would the Teutonic spirit begin to recede?
Back they came, ever more clever
Pegging us back with a goal from Weber

Subsequently, the match went to extra time
Up stepped Hurst, whose name would soon chime
He scored two goals, the second of which
Saw delirious spectators flood onto the pitch

At last, the referee's whistle finally blew
Ramsey's prognostication had come true
Such pandemonium was never witnessed nor seen
As Bobby Moore received the Jules Rimet trophy from our Queen

So well done to Alf Ramsey, Moore, Cohen, the Charlton brothers, Hurst, Ball, Hunt, Stiles, Wilson, Peters and Banks
Congratulations from us all with eternal thanks!

Did Somebody Say, "Just Eat!"

The cupboard is bare. I'm feeling ravenous
My rumbling stomach is truly cavernous
Not a slice of bread nor biscuit in view
I've just discovered; there's no cereal too!

The pangs of hunger are growing stronger
Don't think I can stand this agony much longer
I search the kids' bedrooms. They've got no sweets
No crisps, candies, chocolates or treats!

I could easily eat a "scabby" horse
Laced with lashings of Tabasco sauce
Time to call a family pow-wow
To discuss what we should do right now

Round the table to "chew the fat"
Oh, the irony in saying that!
Choices, Choices. There's no need to tweet
The kids ask, "Did somebody say just eat?"

"Kentucky, McDonalds, Kebab or Domino"
Enough to make the juices flow!
A show of hands reveals the decision
"Domino's" it is, no hoots of derision

Sloppy Guiseppe for me. Margarita for the sprogs
Hawaiian for the missus … but none for the dogs!
We ring for the takeaway, a timely treat
Prayers answered. "Did somebody say just eat?"

I'll Be There

When you wake in the morning with an addled head
And the day fills you with uncertainty and dread
You just can't get into gear
No worries! Reach out, I'll be there

When you can't be bothered to wash or shave
And those infernal kids just won't behave
You gnash your teeth, curse and swear
Stop, ponder, inhale but remember I'll be there

Somehow, you've taken the kids to school
But frustratingly, you still feel like a fool
There are jobs to do, meals to prepare
If you need advice and support, I'll be there

The news is depressing, there's so much turmoil
Your car needs a service and a top-up with oil
You're in desperate need of something to cheer
Close your eyes, look upwards, for I'll be there

You're full of angst and in a dead-end job
Just another cog in the machinery blob
All you crave is a sympathetic ear
You know where I am, I'll empathise. I'll be there

We're on the "road to nowhere" or so say "Talking Heads"
As you pore through your existential shreds
When you find yourself plummeting to the depths of despair
Apply the brakes. Call me. I'll always be there
You're short on money and on the way to the bank
Suddenly the car stops, no petrol in the tank
There are presents to buy with Christmas so near
Let's talk. Pull up a chair, because I'm going nowhere

In time you'll discover that people do care
They recognise your worries and perceive what you fear
With you, they'll share and dry many a tear
Come into my house and we'll say a prayer
All will soon become clear … for you know, I'll be there

Hallowe'en

Fun and frolics or the bane of the lonely?
It's the time of year for the one and only
Yes. Halloween is upon us but what does it mean?
Superstitious nonsense or a played-out scene?

Whatever; the stories are rooted in history
Arcane, dark practices augment the mystery
Some ask, is it just an "Americanism?"
Or part of an established global mechanism

Is it a ritual thought to be Pagan?
With effigies of Thatcher and Reagan?
Inside, somewhere, is a theme solemn and serious
Children don't care. They're naturally curious

Over time the date moved to October's end
Finalised by those who'd researched and penned
The eve before All Souls' Day, holy or hallowed
The latter evolved into Halloween, 'twas crowed

Was it to herald the onset of Winter?
Herds returned from pastures in time for dinner
A time when land tenures were renewed
When hearty potions and ales were brewed

To the present day when parties are staged
Banishing ghosts, ghouls, and phantoms and to keep them caged
Beings such as witches and hobgoblins entered the equation
Together with fairies and demons on such an occasion
An excuse for kids to romp and caper
Before lighting the Jack o'lantern taper
Pumpkins galore, children in disguises
To see off those creatures in all their guises

Youngsters knocking on doors with supervision
Better than staying indoors watching television!
Tricking or treating, asking for candy
The occupants usually have sweet goodies handy!

Tricks include flour and eggs thrown at your pane
Whilst miscreants utter words most profane
It's preferable for us all to bite our tongue
Even when reluctant to join in the fun

It'll soon be over for another year
Even though some still curse and swear
This annual custom will long remain
Like next Fall, when it will happen again!

Global Limericks

An impatient ruler from China
Owned a naughty blackbird, a Mynah
It copied and mimicked
Until its owner reached his limits
And put the damned bird on the next liner!

A meteorologist from India
Had a beautiful wife named Cynthia
He said "Don't go out today
Because the gales will blow you away
And tomorrow will be even windier!"

A smarmy politician from France
Met a debutante belle at a dance
He invited her back to his place
But she soon slapped his face
Adding "You've got to be joking. No chance!"

A prominent Minister in Wales
From the pulpit spewed forth lewd tales
Of debauchery and vice
That were distinctly not nice
Even shocking the congregation of males!

A peasant farmer from Chile
Dressed in clothes that looked quite silly
He went to work in a shirt
That was covered in dirt
But at least the collar was frilly!
A driving instructor from Sweden
Was stopped one day for speedin'
The police were not happy
'Cos this Scandinavian chappy
Gave details which were very misleading!

A Catholic woman in Malta
Got engaged to a chap named Walter
He said, “I’ve set the date
She replied, “I won’t be late”
But left him standing alone at the altar!

A cunning Pharmacist from Russia
Was more than just a pill crusher
He did deals most devious
With folks who had “previous”
Turns out he was a known drug pusher!

A bouzouki player from Greece
Was not one to keep the peace
The neighbours grew wild
And increasingly riled
Shouting “When will your strumming cease?”

A tin pot Dictator from North Korea
Had a hairstyle that looked most queer
Although he looked weird
His people were scared
To question who trimmed his hair!

Save Our Pub!

More than a pint
A place to have fun
There used to be four
Now there's not even one!

What's to happen now?
What do we do?
Not another broken vow
We really haven't a clue!

Call an emergency meeting
Invite the local folk
Ensure there's plenty of seating
Time to go for broke

Canvas opinion and strength of feeling
Fight any development suggestion
There'll be some wheeling and dealing
Of that, there is no question!

Committee formed; a time for steering
Volunteers ready and prepared
This project is a time for daring
Maybe not as bad as first feared?

Money needs raising, as quick as we can
Certificates issued as shares
Sponsors becoming part of the plan
Nowt' gets down if no one dares!
Fingers crossed and with luck on our side
Our aspirations will be realised
We don't want "sharks" taking us for a ride
Con artists are to be despised

Other communities have done a "Lazarus"
And resurrected a dying pub
There's no reason why it cannot be us
With a return to a communal hub

Thort Tongued Chrith

This is a tale about short-tongued Chris who is married to Sharon. The story goes something like this!
They lived in a village near Diss, unlike the Ritz!
"I'm off to work Tharon", said Chris. "Give uth a kith."
She wailed "You've not washed up. I'm not giving you a kiss."
Chris barked back, "Are you taking the pith? Our marriage ith a farth. You can kith my arth!"
Chris left his missus who worked as a Baker.
"Oh, I loathe my job ath a poor thoomaker."
My marriage ith not one of blith. In fact, we've often been on the abyth."
After work, Chris crept back into the house
He was as quiet as the proverbial church mouse
"Wath for dinner Tharon?" meekly asked Chris
"Bread and pullet," back at Chris she did hiss
Chris opined, "I have been rather amith. Perhapth I thould have given Tharon that kith. I gethed that thumthing wath amith!"
Sharon retorted "You never bring me any gifts. To the spare room, you are dismissed!"
Chris figured that with no food in his belly, he'd be better off watching telly.
Thus, in his isolation, as he sat there Chris recalled the words of Freddie Davis who, parrot-faced, shrieked "I'm thick, thick, thick of it up to here!"
Chris watched football; "Ah, my beloved Spurth … can we beat the Chelthee curth?"
He swore and he ranted as his words he did ramble. Chris shouted at the set "Bloody thamble. Watching thuch thite hath left me in thock. Now, the time ith ten o'clock. Thankfully, I've recorded Thongth of praith. I'll watch it to end thith moath dithmal of dayth!"

School Limericks

There was a Maths teacher called Lurch
Stood like a Minister in church
He knew every logarithm
To him, just basic scholarism
But at least he spared us the birch!

A woodwork master known as Chippy
Didn't like it when pupils got lippy
He'd hold his hammer and plane
And utter words most profane
"Pay attention! If not, be a hippy!"

A headmaster referred to as Kraut
Was not one to rant or shout
He took assembly each morning
As the new day was dawning
He loved authority, no doubt!"

A history tutor nicknamed Sid
As behind his desk, he hid
Read aloud from his book
Barely giving us a look
No one could ever be sure what he did!

An eccentric teacher, monikered Hank
Was more than just a funny crank
Waving his arm like a flipper
He was a demon with the slipper
But a decent fellow, to be frank!
An avuncular master known as Decca
Deemed Geography was his Mecca
He had oodles of patience
As he recited the nations
Veritably, a real name checker!"

A French language teacher called Dot
Often put pupils on the spot
She'd ask, "Comment cava?"
To the reply "Nous ne savons pas"
She'd then yell "You lot ought to be shot!"

A Latin tutor labelled as Taff
Was a genial member of the staff
He'd repeat, "Amo, Amas, Amat"
Or something like that
We all thought he was having a laugh!

An English educator, with soubriquet Morry
Always appeared in a hurry
He taught comprehension and language
Whilst scoffing a sandwich
Then out of the room he would scurry

War. What Has Been Learned?

Enemies hover, champing at the bit
Armies massed awaiting their orders
The King's men would have none of it
Repel those Normans from across the channel borders
Arrows flying through the sky
Too late. The King took one in the eye
Perhaps, away, he should have turned
But what have the defenders learned?

Long before, and since, wars have been waged
With degrees of barbarity and hate
Prisoners taken and cruelly caged
Not knowing what would be their fate
Battles played out with weapons fierce
Eye for an eye; Tooth for a tooth
Bodies impaled with armour pierced
Slain in vain? Is that the truth?

History repeating itself again and again
Lessons not heeded from yore
Ships sunk out on the open main
Sailors lost by the score
Those who survived returned to land
Traumatised by what they'd witnessed
Hoping and praying that wars be banned
In reality, those souls are scared witless

Wars fought because religious views vary
Purportedly in God's name
Fighters pressganged with no right of query
All such a crying shame
Jew versus Arab: Russia versus Ukraine
Disputing each side's territory
There'll be no satisfaction, that is plain
In this pursuit of glory

So, who covets war? What does it achieve?
As the pages of yesteryear are turned
Dictators, tyrants, and warmongers all flatter to deceive
Ask yourself, by their actions, what have they learned?

For the Grace of God

You look at me with apparent disdain
As I sit here on this cardboard
In all weather come sun, wind or rain
I apologise that I can't afford hardboard

Tonight, I'll stretch out in this empty shop porch
Crammed inside a tatty sleeping bag
No light, not even a basic torch
Oh, what I would give for a fag!

Walk on by if you must. I'm not here by choice
I've committed neither offence nor crime
I'd plead if only you could hear my voice
"Buddy, can you spare me a dime?"

I could be anywhere, city or town
Invisible to all and sundry
It's no joke when "on your uppers, you're down"
More so in a wealthy country

The night shelter is full, "no room at the inn"
How must Mary and Joseph have felt?
Being impoverished is hardly a sin
Far away from the stockbroker belt

My teeth are chattering, my feet are numb
I'm frozen through to the marrow
I haven't a feeling in my fingers and thumb
Please, God, cart me off in a barrow

Somehow, I make it through the night
A miracle in this season of giving
Another chance to make things right
I'm back in the land of the living!

I'm approached by a man in a pin-striped suit
He thrusts a fiver into my hand
His generosity, to me, is really quite cute
A heartwarming gesture so grand

Then off he went, I guess to his office
Or so I presumed to think
When suddenly he returned with two coffees
One for us both to drink!

After a few minutes, I cheered up no end
To contemplate that someone did care
This man, a real "Samaritan friend"
Spent time when others did not dare

Warmed up, with faith in humanity restored
I collected my belongings and walked
Tonight, there would be no more cardboard
I'm thrilled that, with me, someone talked

Today's the first day of the rest of my life
I've bagged a place at the night shelter
No more will I be cut like a knife
No more existential helter-skelter

So, there for the grace of God go you
Happy with your suburban existence
Slow down, stop, and think of others too
Woe betides living on a pittance!

Jay

Flashing colours gay and vivid
Unlike any other bird of corvid
Rooks, magpies, jackdaws and crows
Jays are most striking as their plumage shows

We don't see you often, maybe once in a while
Maybe you think that, of you, we revile
We have no oak trees with acorns to cache
As for nuts, seeds and suet, we have a stash

You're not here for long as around you do flit
Perhaps rehearsing for a pantomime skit?
No matter, your presence we readily savour
Very much without fear or favour!

Though you may be in search of food
You've very much warmed this author's mood
Undoubtedly, you are a birdwatcher's delight
A joy to behold in hours of daylight

You've had your fill of suet and seed
Just enough to satiate your need
Now you've checked out our garden, please return
We hope that us, you will not spurn

Off you fly to a nearby stump
Audaciously exposing your bold, white, rump
Where you're off to nobody knows
My guess? To join your cousins, the crows!

"I Was Just Thinking of That!"

The last drop of milk, mere remnants of bread
Not even food to offer the cat
I'll have to pop out to the shops instead
All of a sudden cries a voice from the shed
"I was just thinking of that!"

My stomach thinks that my throat has been cut
I'm feeling a bit of a prat
I'll have to drop into Pizza Hut
When that voice cries out "But, but, but"
"I was just thinking of that!"

On the way back, I'll stop at the pub
There's only myself to blame
At least I will have acquired the grub
Lo! That voice shouts out from the bathroom tub
"I was just thinking the same!"

Back home, we tuck into the happy feast
We don't need to use a placemat
That "Margaritha" is a bit of a beast
The voice pipes up "I don't care in the least"
"But it's funny, I was just thinking of that!"

Remember that time at the Christmas bash?
We didn't walk but instead took the bike
On the way home we were involved in a crash
The voice agreed "We were out on the lash
Amazing how great minds think alike!"
And so, this tale reaches its conclusion
You might deem it a load of old tat
If nothing else a rhythmic fusion
The voice agrees, as ever the allusion
For it was just thinking of that!

Good Manners Cost Nowt'

Stand up when a teacher enters the class
No need to scream and shout
He's trying to educate us all, en-masse
Remember! Good manners cost nowt!

What did Akela say when you were a Cub?
As you were cleaning that shelf
Let adults and seniors be first for their grub
Always put others before yourself!

When Granny calls around with goodies, so sweet
Don't loiter like a spoilt young lout
Greet her, take her coat, offer her a seat
Recall what you were taught as a Scout!

When you're with your girl walking down the road
Stand between her and the traffic
She will think such courtesy you showed
Even if others view you as a maverick!

And if the rain suddenly starts to pour
Lend your belle a robust umbrella
For, as you eventually reach her door
She'll note that you're a polite young fellah!

Make sure that she enters first
Basic etiquette when all is said and done
To do otherwise would just look worse
And never refer to her as "hun!"

If others should buy the next round of drinks
For the second time in a row
Rapidly have a genuine rethink
Apologise and say, "Sorry it's my go!"

Never take advantage of mum and dad
They bought your clothes from “Jeff Banks”
Show your gratitude and just be glad
But don’t forget, always say thanks!”

Think back through life’s lessons learned
You’ll soon realise, no doubt
That though many pages were turned
Remember! Good manners cost nowt!

The Delivery Driver

They're everywhere you go these days
Delivering parcels and packets
Their antics never cease to amaze
As they sport their high-visibility jackets

"Package for you love, sign here, please
Hurry up, there's no time to lose"
"Wait a moment, I didn't order cheese
I requested bottles of booze!"

Too late, the driver has departed
Off to the next port of call
You're feeling anything but light-hearted
With this cheddar on the floor in the hall!

The driver is off to town ever so speedy
Running late, with lots to deliver
To the rich, working class, poor and needy
Across the bridge and over the river

He jumps red lights and veers across lanes
As motorists all around are tootin'
He's not bothered. He's off to Staines
Leatherhead, Watford and Luton!

Woe betides pedestrians on pavement or path
He'll park all over the place
Is this guy just having a laugh?
Not so, by the look on his face

Old, young, deaf, blind or unstable
Or simply an unknown stranger
Jump out of the way if you are able
This driver is nothing but danger!

The dark has descended, it's way past six
Lights on, no need to complain
The driver has finished, he's back from the sticks
Until the next day, when it all starts again!

Spartacus Strikes!

Thud, crash, splatter
Raptor causing strife
Victim's heart a 'flutter
Assassin extinguishes life

Talons tearing flesh
Feathers strewn around
Dove in a mess
Deceased on the ground

Birds hiding behind bushes
Fearing brutal Spartacus
As blood gushes
Witnessing slaughter barbarous

Spartacus carries Dove
Under the silver birch
Orphans gaze from above
Safely on their perch

Spartacus' wife arrives
Far bigger than him
Their species thrives
Helping partner keep trim

Mean, keen, killing machine
Visiting most days
My garden to screen
Or simply to gaze?

Devious, stealthy hawk
Designed for hunting prey
No chance to squawk
For those who cross his way

Suddenly Spartacus doth depart
Darting swiftly away
Rapidly, like a beating heart
He'll swoop by another day!

Cricket

It all began way back in the past
Played by gentlemen and those of blue-collar
A truly, strictly, amateur cast
Well-mannered, they did not holler!

W G Grace, eminent all-rounder
Batted and bowled with pride
A sportsman never to flounder
"I'm not out umpire" he cried!

County cricket, the traditionalists' game
Contested with keenness and fervour
Contrasts with chess as exceedingly tame
With cucumber sandwiches, at tea, to savour

A fixture competed for over two innings
Batsmen compiling their score
Bowlers taking wickets to prevent them from winning
In good weather, who could ask for more?

Test cricket, the ultimate sporting battle
Played over a potential five days
England versus Australia tested the mettle
Such skills never cease to amaze!

Other countries gradually entered the fray
Entranced by this intriguing sport
Cricket was definitely here to stay
The "bug" was veritably caught!

Over the decades the sport did change
Oh, the purists vented their spleen!
"ODI's, Twenty-Twenty, The Hundred?" they'd whinge
Such amendments they'd never seen!

Players wearing coloured pyjamas
Fielding restrictions aplenty
Would these amendments really harm us?
Especially in the format, “Twenty-Twenty”

Players enticed by soaring wages
Professionalism entrenched forever
Women now playing on world stages
An advancement of equality, quite clever!

Cavalier approaches, especially in batting
Fours and sixes despatched to all parts
By the likes of Botham, Richards and Gatting
What a way to win our hearts!

The bowlers and fielders we must not forget
Anderson, Trueman, Holding and Broad
True warriors who honed their art in the nets
Putting batsmen “to the sword!”

The spinners also display their guile
Murali, Swann, Rashid and the late, great, Warne
Bamboozling their victims with elaborate style
As the batters’ wickets were shorn!

Fielders, so athletic in moving around
As the captain battens down the hatches
The ball, from the bat, must not go to ground
For, as oft said, “catches win matches!”

Why Do You Lie?

You take us all for fools
You tell many an untruth
You don't play by the rules
Caught out by an amateur sleuth

Your "porkies" know no bounds
At first, I laugh and then I cry
You saw a fox chasing the hounds
Just another crass, absurd, lie

You say you'll be back in time for dinner
I've heard that said many times before
You must think I'm an absolute beginner
As you roll home in the morning at four

Did you treat your marriage vows as serious
When you pledged in front of the Vicar?
Gradually your motives became mysterious
Not good for your loved one's ticker!

It's clear something's wrong, plainly amiss
With your regular inconsistent tales
You were seen in town, giving that guy a kiss
When you told us you were working in Wales!

We've all had enough. Time for a change
As I look heavenwards up to the sky
Your life, you'll have to rearrange.
But why do you have to lie?

The Lurking Assassin

Pulling, stabbing, tearing
Attritional, eroding, shearing
Constant, nagging pain
Sadly, no gain

Ribcage feeling sore
How much more?
Struggling for breath
What's next? Death?

Speak to mother
Wait, don't bother
Regrettably, she's deceased
Death is a beast

Pain still there
Can't get into gear
Need medical assistance
Break this resistance

First a prayer
To the Lord up there
Please allay my distress
I'm in a mess

Read a Gospel
Prior to hospital
Words of solace
Comfortingly flawless
Ambulance duly arrives
Before health nosedives
Thorough examination conducted
Paramedics impeccably unflustered

Heart irregularity detected
Hopefully not infected
Hospital incredibly busy
Feeling nauseatingly dizzy

More investigations ordered
Experience is awkward
Bloods, X-rays, scans
What further plans?

Potent opiates given
Floating off to heaven
Wait another hour
Faces glower

Don’t want to weep
Let me sleep
Suddenly Consultant appears
Allaying my fears

Condition deemed treatable
Nothing is unbeatable
Situation not minor
Diagnosis? Unstable angina!

And Then She Was Gone

We thought, nay believed, you'd be here forever
We wished not for those ties to sever
Aged 96, with 70 years at the helm
You'd overseen the enormity of your realm
Though your demise was ruefully inevitable
For many, your passing was unintelligible.

No longer will we be beguiled
By the million times you smiled
You had patience and forbearance at all times
Never once did you fluff your lines
Lessons from you we could all learn
Like children in class awaiting their turn

We witnessed the Trooping of the colour on Horse Guards' parade
When exemplary behaviour you always displayed
There seemed almost an uncanny alchemy
As you galvanised those to whom you waved from the balcony
Your subjects gathered at the Palace railing
Clapping, cheering, singing and wailing

You met Prime Ministers galore in your reign
Presidents and Monarchs from America to Spain
Banquets, feasts, ceremonies, parties in the garden
You would never need to use your Royal Pardon
State opening of Parliament with your regal speech
Delivered exquisitely, a perfect peach
Your sense of humour never failed to amuse
A facet you, not once, would lose
You said that "you had to be seen to be believed"
If not, perhaps others might have felt aggrieved
And rather than express anything to the contrary
You simply stated that "recollections may vary"

Your Royal mantra was "Never complain, never explain"
Quite simply this motto will, forever, remain
No sane being would challenge our Ruler
Not in days of yore, under the House of Tudor!
Your authority was complete and absolute
Even at meetings of many an Institute

As your health gradually faltered
Never did you want your schedule altered
Each day you read Government despatches
Of which there were many batches
Your last Prime Minister was Truss
You greeted her at Balmoral, no fuss!

The world was then stunned, as days later
Sad news hit us, like a giant freighter
You were called by your divine creator
Tidings to stun even the sturdiest Quaker
A mourning period ensued, most reverent and solemn
Even Nelson would have been moved as your funeral cortege passed by his stately column

You had lain in state at Westminster Hall
As people filed past from as far as Nepal
Your son, our King, now assumes your mantle
A position he acceded to, one he can handle
We'll never forget you Ma'am, you were unique
For now, Charles will cope. He has the technique!

Crazy PC World!

The world has gone political correctness mad
Does this make you feel bad, sad or glad?
These days we dare not risk to offend
Is it safe to opine? Where will it all end?

We all laughed at the Punch and Judy show
"That's the way to do it!"
Now it's depicted as abusive. Oh no!
Kids watching before didn't care one bit!

Who remembers Captain Pugwash with Seaman Stains?
Cleverly crafted animation
Removed from broadcast due to smutty innuendo contained
What's happening to the nation?

You can't watch "Til death us do part" anymore
With Alf calling his missus "Silly old moo"
If he showed bias now, he'd be shown the door
Another series no longer to view

"Love thy neighbour", another programme
With white against black in racial banter
Censored by the restriction gang
Taken off our screens at a canter

You can no longer say "Nancy boy" or "Dyke"
We must accept that it takes all sorts
If you don't, you'll have to get on your bike
And keep to yourself your thoughts!
Us men cannot use a wolf whistle
Should we see a pretty woman in the street
You'd never hear the end of the epistle
With your face turned "white as a sheet!"

You can't "fat shame" someone with excess pounds
Or use vocabulary like Porky, Titch or Lanky
Such folk are presumed mortified by such sounds
Isn't it all, perhaps, a bit too cranky?"

A psychotic patient goaded his nurse
Saying "You don't like me, do you?"
The nurse without having to swear or curse
Replied "I'm here to simply treat you. If only you knew!"

A black man in a wheelchair waited at the pharmacy desk
He told the female assistant "You look more beautiful than ever"
The assistant retorted "You are a sex pest
I can report your comments. Isn't that clever?"

God help you if you're referred to as old
Ageism went out with the Ark
Who wants to be left out in the cold?
Or left fumbling around in the dark?
Let's respect each other without fear
And acknowledge each other as unique
Go about your business with a conscience clear
That's it. Now enjoy your week!

Strictly

The "Beeb" produced a winner back in 2004
Possibly the greatest show you ever saw
Celebrity partnered with a professional
Being taught modern, Latin and ballroom traditional

A programme compered initially by Sir Bruce
He knew how to converse and schmooze
He introduced each couple with zeal
Wanting their scores to be fair but real

Hard work for all the dancers
Some celebrities were basic prancers
Training resulting in toil, sprains and many a blister
Rehearsing to songs on the radio transistor

Professionals include Nikita, Nadia, Vito and Luba
Performing to numbers played sometimes on Tuba!
Partnering with their celebrities around the dance floor
Leaving the audience calling out for more

Performances discussed with Claudia and Tess
Who assured them that they'd done their best
Then the dreaded critique and scores from the judges
Surely, they would hold no grudges?

Fair balanced comments from Shirley, Motsi and Anton
Would leave them feeling far from forlorn
Not so with Craig who said "You could have been faster.
Frankly, darling, that effort was a disaster!"
Dances include Tango, Waltz, Rumba and Jive
Surely the latter would score more than a 5?
Anton gets excited when he spots a "fleckle"
He'll purr with delight, but certainly not heckle

As the weeks evolve and competition gets stiffer
The judges demand more, and their views may differ
"Celebs" do well to get to the Blackpool Tower
By now, their confidence does truly flower

Not long to Christmas and the grand finale
Let's hope the couples have not done badly
They don't want to miss steps or sustain a fall
Not when they're in pursuit of the glitterball!

Finally, a tribute to good old Len
He encouraged the underdog again and again
He knew the true meaning of ambience
And what it meant to be called deserved champions!

The Rhyme of the Modern Matelot

We ventured forth from Solent Sound
On benign waters, thousands milling around
We waved farewell to the cheering throng
Whilst the band played on…and on…and on

Around the Isle of Wight, we did sail
Many passengers by now ashen and pale
Drinks served by anonymous waiters
Enigmatically garbed in Sou'westers and gaiters!

We dined at the top table that night
The captain greeted us before the feast
His hideous grin was a gruesome sight
He cared not a jot in the least

He regaled us with tales most stark
The stories were recounted with candour
Where would we be after dark?
Something we had not planned for

We had no appetite for food
The venison looked quite sorry
Some of us ate, lest we appeared rude
Would we later have need to worry?

The drinks included lashings of wine
Cocktails, spirits, liqueurs in abundance
After the repast would be ballroom time
Would it be formal or a fun dance?

As we awoke the following morning
Many passengers suffered diarrhoea
Alas, there was no prior warning
The symptoms were utterly severe

We chugged through the Channel into Biscay
People vomiting hither and thither
We wondered if in our cabins we should stay
As our bodies began to wither

The ship drifted past Portugal and Spain
Out into the Atlantic
By now storms were preceded by rain
All around were becoming frantic

The crew were looking "green at the gills"
Persevering with their tasks
Some joined the litany of ills
After imbibing from their casks

Lo, we navigated the Strait of Gibraltar
Proceeding eastwards across the Med
Now we were reciting verses from our Psalter
Many of us were now abed

As we headed for Greece the situation was grave
The ship's Padre was summoned often
We prayed to the Lord that us he would save
And that the blow to us all he might soften

Greece emerged and into Port Piraeus
The captain, by now gaunt and fatigued
We'd move on, he didn't wish to delay us
By this point, we were more than intrigued

The ship made its way to Africa's shore
Egypt, Port Said, to be exact
Spontaneously, passengers lurched to the floor
As their remaining strength was sapped

No one was desirous of leaving the vessel
Such was the general uncertainty
We struggled to sit aside a trestle
Owing to the potent Burgundy

After a day of purgatory, we set off for Israel
Bound for the destination of Ashdod
An overnight passage that mightn't go well
Would we survive this travail, please God?

Armed security guards met us on board
Demanding to peruse our documents
Although their request could not be ignored
We had no wish to view Jewish monuments

Bethlehem and Jerusalem had been on the agenda
For travellers trepidatious but bold
Most of us were about to surrender
It transpired that the seer had foretold

That evening to Turkey we were bound
In danger up to our necks
Would our craft be run aground?
The crew were in lifejackets on decks

The ship teetered on ferocious waves
Rocking all over the main
Some thought the crew acted like knaves
It was mused, had the captain a brain?

Hope was plummeting as our ship was tilted
We sloped at a grotesque angle
Passengers' bodies at this juncture had wilted
Twisted, contorted, thrust through a mangle

Our fate was sealed by the Katabatic
A freak wind sending us under
We'd succumbed to matters of the climatic
Driven below by storms and thunder

We made our entreaties to our maker
Resigning ourselves to dark gloom
For the ship, nothing could save her
Interred in the ocean's vague womb